Destination Detectives

Germany

North America

Europe

Asia

GERMANY

Africa

South America

Australasia

Sonja Schanz and Gerry Donaldson

www.raintreepublishers.co.uk

Visit our website to find out more information about **Raintree** books.

To order:
☎ Phone 44 (0) 1865 888112
📄 Send a fax to 44 (0) 1865 314091
💻 Visit the Raintree Bookshop at **www.raintreepublishers.co.uk** to browse our catalogue and order online.

First published in Great Britain by Raintree,
Halley Court, Jordan Hill, Oxford OX2 8EJ,
Part of Harcourt Education.
Raintree is a registered trademark of
Harcourt Education Ltd.

Produced for Raintree Publishers by Discovery Books Ltd
Editorial: Kathryn Walker, Sonya Newland,
Melanie Waldron and Lucy Beevor
Design: Gary Frost and Rob Norridge
Picture Research: Amy Sparks
Production: Duncan Gilbert
Originated by Modern Age
Printed and bound in China
By South China Printing Company

10 digit ISBN 1 4062 0722 5
13 digit ISBN 978 1 4062 0722 4
10 9 8 7 6 5 4 3 2 1
11 10 09 089 07

10 digit ISBN 1 4062 0729 2
13 digit ISBN 978 1 4062 0729 3
10 9 8 7 6 5 4 3 2 1
11 10 09 08 07

British Library Cataloguing in Publication Data
Schanz, Sonja
Germany. - (Destination detectives)
1.Germany - Geography - Juvenile literature 2.Germany -
Social life and customs - 21st century - Juvenile
literature 3.Germany - Civilization - Juvenile literature
I.Title
943'.0882

This levelled text is a version of *Freestyle:
Destination Detectives: Germany*, produced for Raintree
Publishers by White-Thomson Publishing Ltd.

Acknowledgements
Corbis pp. 6b (Régis Bossu/Sygma), 18 (Richard Klune),
20 (Dave G. Houser/Post-Houserstock), 21 (Adam
Woolfitt), 31 (Inge Yspeert), 34-35 (Michaela Rehle/
Reuters), 36 (Régis Bossu/Sygma); Getty Images pp. 5b
(Sean Gallup), 26 (Sean Gallup), 37 (Kati Jurischka/
Bongarts); Photolibrary pp. 4 (The Travel Library
Limited), 5 (Japack Photo Library), 5t (Workbook, Inc.),
5m (Robin Smith), 6t (Panstock Llc Catalogue),
8-9 (Photononstop), 9 (Mauritius Die Bildagentur Gmbh),
10-11 (Jon Arnold Images), 12-13 (Ifa-Bilderteam Gmbh),
13 (Photolibrary.Com), 14 (Photolibrary.Com),
17 (Jon Arnold Images), 19 (Robin Smith), 22 (Mauritius
Die Bildagentur Gmbh), 23 (Robert Harding Picture Library
Ltd), 24-25 (Jon Arnold Images), 25 (Plainpicture),
27 (Index Stock Imagery), 28 (Jon Arnold Images),
29 (Robin Smith), 30 (Monsoonimages), 32 (Mauritius
Die Bildagentur Gmbh), 32-33 (Index Stock Imagery),
33 (Jon Arnold Images), 38 (Index Stock Imagery),
41t (Monsoonimages), 42 (The Travel Library Limited),
43 (Ifa-Bilderteam Gmbh); TopFoto pp. 11 (Michael
Rhodes), 12, 15, 16 (Peter Kingsford), 34 (Keystone),
39 (Ray Roberts), 40 (Keystone), 41b (Harold Chapman).

Cover photograph of German houses reproduced with
permission of Photolibrary/Photononstop.

Contents

Any words appearing in the text in bold, **like this,** are explained in the glossary. You can also look out for them in the Word Bank box at the bottom of each page.

Festivals

Germany has festivals all through the year. Small cities or towns often act out scenes from their past. Rothenburg is a small city that has lots of festivals.

The sound of bells wake you up. It is exactly 8 a.m. The bells are playing a sweet tune.

You look out of your window. There's a crowd in the square below. They are all looking up at a tall building. There's a clock on the front of it. This is where the sound is coming from.

Windows on each side of the clock open. Mechanical figures appear. Some are soldiers. A figure of a smiling man appears last. He drinks from a giant glass. Then the windows close.

Germany is famous for its Christmas markets. They are held in cities such as Frankfurt.

A medieval town

You want to find out more about this clock. So you go down into the square. Suddenly you hear the sound of drums and marching. A troop of soldiers appear. They are dressed like the figures on the clock.

You notice a banner in the square. It says "Festival Rothenburg". So that's where you are! This is Germany. You are in the old city of Rothenburg.

Find out later...

...where you can find this fairy-tale castle.

...why cycling is so popular in Germany.

...which building is known as the "washing machine".

> The city of Rothenburg was founded in 1195. Some of its buildings are hundreds of years old.

medieval belonging to the Middle Ages. This was a period of history between 500 and 1,000 years ago.

You look at a map of Germany. You see that Rothenburg is right in the middle of the country. It looks as if Germany has lots of different landscapes.

Germany at a glance

SIZE: 357,000 square kilometres (138,000 square miles)

CAPITAL: Berlin

POPULATION: 82.4 million

OFFICIAL LANGUAGE: German

CURRENCY: Euro €

The Black Forest is an area of low hills and woodland. It is great for walking and cycling.

Germany is a major producer of cars. The city of Stuttgart is the home of Mercedes–Benz and Porsche.

WORD BANK   port place where ships load and unload goods or passengers

Hamburg is one of the most important **ports** in Europe. Ships load and unload here.

The Baltic Sea area attracts lots of tourists. The coastline and islands are very beautiful.

Berlin is the German capital. It has many museums and concert halls. Berlin is home to the German **government** (leaders).

Germany is made up of sixteen **states**. These are areas that make some of their own laws. Bavaria is the largest state.

The mountains and lakes of the Alps offer some of the most amazing scenery in Germany.

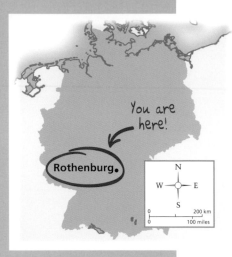

You are here!

Rothenburg

N
W — E
S

0   200 km
0   100 miles

It's a perfect day for a walk in the hills. You decide to explore the area around Rothenburg (see map on left). The River Tauber flows below the town. There are wooded hills and mountains all around.

The German landscape

Large parts of central Germany look like this. But some places have much higher mountains. The Central Uplands is an area north of

Bavaria is in southern Germany. The snow can be deep here. Sometimes people travel across it on skis.

▼

Germany's climate

Germany has a moderate **climate**. This means that periods of cold or hot weather do not usually last long. The coastal areas have warm summers and mild winters. Away from the coast the winters are colder. The summers there are hotter.

  WORD BANK   climate pattern of weather in an area

Rothenburg (see map, page 7). It has mountains more than 1,000 metres (3,000 feet) high. In winter, the higher peaks are covered in snow. People come here for skiing.

There are hardly any mountains in north Germany. There are the Harz Mountains. But apart from them, the land is low and flat.

These are beach baskets. They are called *Strandkörbe*. They protect people from the sun and wind.

Two coastlines

Northern Germany has two stretches of coastline. One is along the North Sea. The other is along the Baltic Sea (see map, page 7).

Views of Germany

You decide to see more of Germany's landscapes. Rothenburg is on a route called the Romantic Road (see map on left). The Romantic Road runs to the south of Germany. You take a bus trip along it.

The journey takes all day. But there's so much to look at. Along the way you pass walled towns. They are hundreds of years old. The walls were built to protect the towns from attack.

The Romantic Road

The Romantic Road is 360 kilometres (224 miles) long. It runs from Würzburg to Füssen. The scenery along the way is very beautiful. This is how the road got its name.

The Romantic Road starts in the city of Würzburg.

The amazing Alps

You travel through the ancient city of Augsburg (see map, page 10). After this the land becomes flat. It is perfect for bike riding.

In the distance you can see the Alps. Their mountain tops are covered in snow. Your journey ends in Füssen. The Alps tower over this region.

▲ The Zugspitze is the highest mountain in Germany. It is in the German Alps.

Germany's castles

Almost every region of Germany has beautiful castles. They are often built on top of hills. Sometimes they are built on mountainsides.

Ludwig II

Ludwig II (below) was king of Bavaria from 1864 to 1886. Ludwig wasn't very interested in **government**. He preferred music and buildings.

In 1886 the German government said that Ludwig was mad. He died a few days later. Some people believe he was murdered.

You visit the fairy-tale castle of Neuschwanstein. This is near Füssen (see map, page 7). The castle was built for King Ludwig II.

The German Empire

Germany was once lots of smaller regions. These were known as **states**. Each state had its own ruler. Bavaria was a state. Ludwig II was king of Bavaria. The most powerful state was Prussia. Its ruler was King Wilhelm.

WORD BANK   chancellor chief minister

In 1871 all the states were joined together. The new country was known as the German Empire. Wilhelm became its emperor (ruler). Berlin became its capital city. The empire lasted until the end of World War I. This was in 1918.

End of the Empire

After 1918, Germany became poor. Many people had no jobs. They had no money. Life was very hard for many German people.

This is the castle at Neuschwanstein. It was the model for Sleeping Beauty's castle at Disneyland.

Otto von Bismarck

Otto von Bismarck (above) was prime minister of Prussia. It was his idea to **unite** (join) the different states. Bismarck became Germany's first chancellor, or leader. The country became very powerful under Bismarck.

unite join together

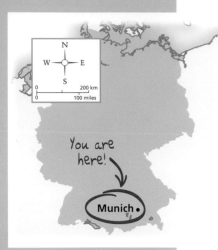

You are here!

Munich

World War II

You travel to Munich (see left). This is a lively city. It is famous for its beer festival.

At Munich you find out about Adolf Hitler. In the 1920s, Hitler became a leader in Germany. He was the leader of the Nazi Party. Hitler first gathered support in Munich. He promised to make Germany strong again.

Hitler became **chancellor** (leader) in 1933. In 1939 he led Germany into World War II. Hitler was defeated in 1945. Germany was then divided into East Germany and West Germany.

This picture shows Adolf Hitler (centre) at a **rally** in 1934. This was a huge meeting of his supporters.

East and West

East Germany and West Germany were two countries (see map, page 24). West Germany became the richer country. Many East Germans moved there.

The city of Berlin was inside East Germany. But it was also divided into East and West. The East Germans built a wall through Berlin. The wall stopped East Germans moving to the West. Guards shot at anyone who tried to climb over the wall.

In 1989 the wall was opened. People began to tear it down. In 1990 the two Germanys were **united** (joined together) again.

The Berlin Wall was broken down in 1989. German people could move again from East to West.

You decide to visit Cologne (see map, page 7). You go to the main railway station in Munich. You climb on board an Inter City Express (ICE) train.

ICE trains are fast and comfortable. They connect all Germany's major cities. Other trains travel to the smaller towns and villages.

Traffic on the Rhine

For the last part of your journey, the train runs close to the River Rhine. There are many enormous **barges** on the Rhine. These are flat-bottomed boats. They are carrying goods. They carry them to other parts of Germany. They also carry them to other countries in Europe.

Inland ports

Germany's main **ports** include Berlin, Stuttgart, Cologne, and Dresden (see map, page 7). Ports are places where ships load and unload. But some of these ports are hundreds of miles from the sea.

An ICE train pulls into the main station at Cologne.

WORD BANK   barge flat-bottomed boat used for transporting goods

This barge is travelling on the River Rhine. It is passing by the city of Cologne.

Barges or lorries?

Why are barges a popular way for carrying goods? Trucks can travel quicker than barges. But a modern barge can deliver 50 times more goods than a single truck. It also causes less **pollution**.

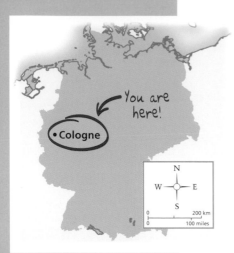

You are here!

• Cologne

N
W — E
S

0   200 km
0   100 miles

City transport

You can see Cologne Cathedral in the distance. You see its famous twin spires (see photo on page 17). The train pulls into the city's main station.

It is very easy to get about Cologne (see map on left). There are plenty of buses and **trams**. There are also underground trains.

You only need one ticket for a trip across town. You can use this on buses, trams, and trains.

Many German cities have trams. Trams help keep pollution levels down.

WORD BANK   tram   train that runs on rails through city streets

By bike or on foot

Cycling in the cities is very safe. There are special lanes for bike riders. The German **government** encourages people to use public transport or bikes. This reduces the **pollution** caused by cars.

It is also easy to get around cities on foot. Most city centres are free or partly free of traffic.

Sharing costs

It is becoming popular to share car journeys in Germany. Organizations help bring together people who are making the same trip. This means it costs less for the drivers. It also reduces the number of cars on the road.

This is a street in Frankfurt (see map, page 7). Many German cities have bike lanes next to traffic lanes.

pollution release of harmful chemicals or waste into air, water, or soil

Eating and drinking

Sausages

There is an amazing choice of sausages in Germany. Each region produces special sausages. Some of them are huge. They can be 1 metre (3 feet) long!

Strolling around Cologne makes you hungry. There are plenty of restaurants and cafés here. You decide to try traditional German food. You buy a sausage from a stall. It is served with mustard and a bread roll.

Bread and meat

Afterwards you go into a bakery. There is a huge choice of breads and rolls. There are all kinds of cakes and pastries, too. You buy yourself a delicious cake.

Sausages are a favourite food in Germany.

Many different meats are available in Germany. They include several types of cold meats. There are hundreds of different sausages. You'll see some odd-looking special meats, too. One of them is pigs' feet.

Coffee and cake

Older Germans like to meet up with friends or family in the afternoon. They meet for a cup of coffee and a cake. Many people get together like this every week.

People meet at a café in Regensburg. This is in the **state** of Bavaria (see map, page 7).

The ice-cream parlour

Young people in Germany enjoy meeting up for an ice-cream. There are many small ice-cream parlours to choose from.

Fresh food

There are some giant supermarkets in Germany. But most people prefer to buy fresh food each day. They get fresh bread from the baker's shop each morning. Many towns have an outdoor market. These are good places for fresh fruit and vegetables.

Almost every town and village in Germany has its own market.

Favourite dishes

At home, families usually eat a variety of food. They eat German food and food from around the world. There's plenty of choice if you want to eat out, too. Turkish and Italian restaurants are very popular. This is because many Italian and Turkish people have come to live in Germany.

Cologne's squares are filled with restaurants and cafés.

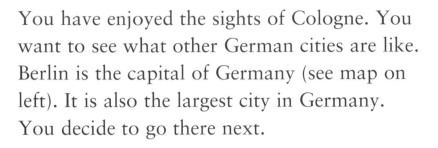

City life

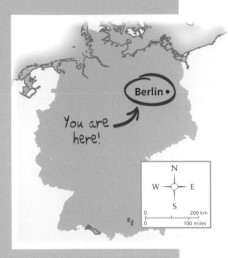

You have enjoyed the sights of Cologne. You want to see what other German cities are like. Berlin is the capital of Germany (see map on left). It is also the largest city in Germany. You decide to go there next.

The capital

Your train pulls into Berlin's new station. This is the largest train station in Europe. Trains running from the north of Europe to the south stop here. They meet trains running from western to eastern Europe.

Families divided

The Berlin Wall divided Berlin from 1961 to 1989. West Berlin belonged to West Germany. But it was like an island in East Germany (see map below). The wall separated families and friends.

The main station is at the edge of a huge park. This is named the Tiergarten. Berliners love to walk or bike here. Some just come here to sit.

You saw a similar park in the centre of Munich. That was called the Englischer Garten (English Garden). Lots of German people choose to live in the centre of a city. These parks mean they have green space close by.

Germans enjoy watersports at the Wannsee lakes in Berlin.

The Tiergarten in Berlin is a huge green space. It is in the middle of the city.

Berlin's beaches

Berlin has its own beaches. These are mainly at the Wannsee. This is an area with two large lakes. The Wannsee is a short train journey from the centre of Berlin.

Rebuilding Berlin

After the war, large parts of Berlin had to be rebuilt. East and West Berlin became two separate cities.

Berlin was **reunited** (joined together again) in 1990. The German **government** (leaders) moved there in 1991. This meant that many new buildings were needed. Some old buildings were restored.

Many centres

Berlin is different from many other capital cities. It is not the place where everything important in the country happens.

Some people call the Chancellory the "Washing Machine". This is because of its colour and shape!

WORD BANK government group of people that makes laws and manages the country

For example, Frankfurt am Main (see map, page 7) is Germany's financial centre. Many banks have headquarters there. Germany's largest university is in Munich. Other cities have world-famous museums and galleries.

Music centre

Berlin is very popular with young people. Lots of big concerts are held here. Berlin also has many nightclubs.

The Sony Centre is in Berlin. It contains shops and offices. It also has restaurants and museums.

Hamburg

You are here!

Hamburg

Hamburg (see map on left) is Germany's second-largest city. It is a very old city. People first settled there more than 1,100 years ago.

Hamburg is on the River Elbe. About 1.7 million people live in the city. But Hamburg is a very large city. It never seems overcrowded.

Hamburg festivals

Hamburg has several festivals. There are music festivals and street festivals. Filmfest Hamburg is one of the most important. This film festival is held in September.

The **port** of Hamburg lies on the River Elbe. The Elbe flows into the North Sea.

A city by the sea

Hamburg is one of the world's greatest seaports. This is where ships load and unload. Hamburg has some fine old buildings. Many are made from red brick. They have very steep roofs.

You go to the famous fish market. It takes place every Sunday. The market closes late in the morning. This is so people can go to church.

In Hamburg many people go to St. Michael's. This is a beautiful old cathedral.

Religion in Germany

Christianity is the main religion in Germany. It is based on the teachings of Jesus Christ.

One of Germany's greatest cathedrals is in Cologne (see map, page 7).

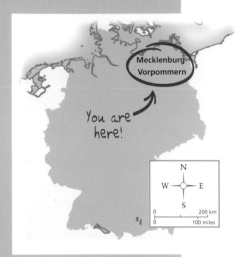

What is life like for people in Germany's **rural** (countryside) areas? You decide to find out. You visit the Mecklenburg-Vorpommern region (see map on left).

The countryside here is flat. This is very different from the south. The roads are long and straight. They are lined with trees.

Farming

This is a farming region. People here live in small villages. Many young people have moved out of the area. They have moved to the cities. There is more work there.

Village life

Small German towns and villages have lots of clubs. These clubs offer all sorts of activities. People enjoy getting together in this way. There are also lots of choirs (singing groups).

Germany is one of the largest milk producers in Europe.

WORD BANK   rural to do with the countryside

Fishing

Germany has two coastlines (see map, page 7). One is along the Baltic Sea. The other coastline is along the North Sea. Fishing is an important industry (type of work) all along the coast.

Tourism

The area on the Baltic Sea is very beautiful. It has become popular with tourists. Lots of new hotels have been built on the Baltic coast. They have also been built on the islands off the coast.

Tourism creates many jobs for local people. But it can spoil the peacefulness of an area.

Farming products

Germany's main farming products are:

- milk
- cereals
- meat.

Farms near cities often grow fruit and vegetables. They can sell these at local markets (see below).

Hi-tech farming

You visit one of the farms in this region. There is a lot of machinery here. The pigs are not fed by hand any more. A computer operates their feeding system.

Farm machinery does work that people used to do. Because of this there are fewer jobs in the countryside. This is one reason why young people are moving to the cities.

These people are cycling through the German countryside. The field is full of oil-seed plants.

It is hard for small farms to make enough money. Farms usually need to be large. Small farms usually fail.

Village homes

The villages used to be where farming people lived. Today the villages are homes to people who work in nearby towns. This is because it is cheaper to live in the countryside.

This is a vineyard in the Mosel region.

Vineyards

Germany produces a lot of wine. There are three main wine-producing regions. They are the Rhine, Mosel, and Main regions (see map, page 7).

It's time to head back to Berlin. You want to find out more about the German people. You want to know more about everyday life in Germany.

In Berlin you see children in the streets at 7.15 a.m. This seems early. But in Germany the school day begins at 7.30 or 7.45 a.m.

School life

German children have to go to school between the ages of 6 and 15. They first go to primary school.

First day of school

Germans celebrate a child's first day of school. Parents or friends give the child a *Schultüte*. This is a big cardboard cone (see below). It is filled with sweets. It also contains school items, such as a pen and a pencil case.

At the age of 10 they move on to a secondary school. They can leave full-time school at 15. But then they must study part-time until they are 18.

Many students leave at 15 or 16. They spend three years on a training scheme. This helps them learn skills they need for jobs. Others stay in school full-time until they are 18. They go on to university.

English-speakers

You chat with some students. Most of them speak English very well. German children start learning English at primary school.

School years

There are three different types of secondary school in Germany. The highest level is known as the Gymnasium. After 8 or 9 years at a Gymnasium, students take an exam. This is so they can go on to university.

◄ German secondary schools normally have about 30 students in a class.

Asylum seekers

An **asylum seeker** is someone who leaves their own country. They leave because they are badly treated. After World War II, Germany allowed all asylum seekers in. But in the 1990s, huge numbers of people came to live in Germany. Today, fewer people are allowed in.

Immigrants

A lot of **immigrants** have come to Germany. Many immigrants and their children continue living here. They make up 9 percent of the German population. Immigrants are people who have left their homes in other countries.

Need for workers

The first immigrants came to Germany in the 1950s and 1960s. There was a lot of work in Germany at that time. But there were not enough Germans to do the work. Germany needed these immigrants.

In the early 1990s, special centres were set up for asylum seekers. These centres helped them find places to live.

immigrant someone who moves to another country because they are treated badly in their own country

Different cultures

Immigrants have changed life in Germany. They have brought their own ways of life with them. Today you can eat all kinds of foods in Germany. You can keep healthy with Chinese exercise. You can even learn to play African drums.

Turkish settlers
About a quarter of Germany's immigrants come from the country of Turkey.

Chinese forms of exercise are popular in Germany. These women are doing Tai Chi. This exercise involves slow, graceful movements.

asylum seeker someone who moves to another country because they are treated badly in their own country

Dancing

Dancing is very popular in Germany. Lots of people go to dance schools. Here they learn many dances. They can learn the waltz and the tango. They can learn disco dancing and salsa.

Leisure time

Germans spend their free time in lots of different ways. Many shops are not allowed to open on Sundays. But the city centres are not empty. People go to the cafés. Some go to museums. Sunday is also a day for visiting family and friends.

These people are enjoying a walk through the countryside. They are in Bavaria (see map, page 7).

➤

A passion for health

Lots of people enjoy a Sunday walk. They go walking in the park or woods. Others jog or cycle through the forests.

Many Germans are interested in health and fitness. They also like to relax. **Spas** are very popular. Spas are places that offer special health treatments. These treatments include baths in spring water or mud.

Visit a spa

Many towns in Germany have a name that begins with "Bad". This is German for "bath" or "spa".

Baden Baden is Germany's most famous spa town. These people are bathing in warm spring water.

spa place offering health treatment. Many spas are near a spring or by the sea.

Everywhere you go in Germany, you see litter bins in different colours. What are they for?

Recycling

These bins are for different types of rubbish. Drinks cans go into one type of bin. Waste paper goes into another. Even houses have more than one bin. The waste must be separated. This is so it can be **recycled**.

Germany is trying to protect the environment in many ways. Recycling is one way. Recycling means reusing waste. This helps to reduce **pollution**.

Most homes in Germany use special bins, like this. They are for separating the waste. ▶

WORD BANK recycle to break down waste materials and use them to make new products

Cleaner air

Cars are a major cause of air pollution in Germany. The **government** is working to solve this problem.

They have made new laws. They make it expensive to drive the cars that cause most pollution. More Germans are now driving **eco-friendly** cars. These are cars that cause less damage to the **environment**.

This is a Smart car. It is a small, eco-friendly car.

Saving the forests

Germany is famous for its forests. But in the late 1970s, the forests began to die. Air pollution was killing them. New laws (rules) were made. These reduced the pollution caused by industries and cars.

pollution release of harmful chemicals or waste into air, water, or soil

Stay or go?

You've seen some amazing places in Germany. But there are still lots of things left to see. What will you do? Will you stay or go home?

Still to see and do

Dresden (see map, page 7) was one of Europe's most beautiful cities. But its centre was mostly destroyed in World War II. Some of Dresden's famous buildings have been rebuilt. You could take a boat there. You could travel down the River Elbe.

This is the New Palace in Potsdam. It is just one of the city's amazing palaces.

Potsdam (see map, page 7) is famous for its beautiful palaces and lakes. The city of Potdsam is just outside Berlin.

If you feel brave you could head to Brocken. This is in the Harz Mountains. People say that witches gather there. Many tourists go to the Harz Mountains. They go there to enjoy the beautiful scenery and towns.

Who speaks German?

German is the main language of Austria (see map, page 7). It is also the language of 65 percent of Swiss people. German is also spoken in Luxembourg, Belgium, and parts of northern Italy.

You could take a ride on an old steam train through the Harz Mountains.

World Wide Web

If you want to find out more about Germany, you can search the Internet. Try using keywords such as these:

- Germany
- Berlin
- River Rhine

You can also find your own keywords by using words from this book. Try using a search directory such as www.yahooligans.com

Are there ways for a Destination Detective to find out more about Germany? Yes! Check out the books listed below:

Further reading

Germany (Letters from Around the World), Cath Senker (Evans Publishing, 2005)

Nations of the World: Germany, Greg Nickles (Raintree, 2003)

Take Your Camera: Germany, Ted Park (Raintree, 2004)

The Changing Face of Germany, Sonja Schanz (Raintree, 2002)

The Fall of the Berlin Wall, Patricia Levy (Raintree, 2002)

The Rhine, Ronan Foley (Hodder Wayland, 2005)

WORD BANK Catholic a part of the Christian Church. The Pope is the head of the Roman Catholic Church.

Timeline

1455
Johann Gutenberg publishes the first printed book in Mainz, Germany. This book is the Bible.

1517
Martin Luther protests against the **Catholic** Church in Wittenburg. His protest eventually leads to the formation of the **Protestant** Church.

1835
The first railway opens in Germany.

1871
The German **states** are **united** under Wilhelm of Prussia. The German Empire is created.

1918
Germany is defeated in World War I.

1920s
Economic (money) crisis in Germany. Many people do not have jobs.

1933
Adolf Hitler becomes **chancellor** of Germany. He is the head of the Nazi Party.

1936
The Olympic Games are held in Berlin.

1938
Jewish people and Jewish property are attacked all over Germany.

1939
Germany invades Poland. World War II begins.

1945
Germany is defeated in World War II. The country is divided into East Germany and West Germany.

1949
Bonn becomes the capital of West Germany.

1961
Work begins on the Berlin Wall.

1989
The Berlin Wall is pulled down. East and West Germany are **reunited**.

1990
Germany is officially reunited as one country.

1991
The capital of the united Germany moves back to Berlin.

2002
The Euro becomes Germany's currency.

2006
Angela Merkel becomes Germany's first woman chancellor.

Protestant a part of the Christian Church. Protestants separated from the Catholic Church in the 16th century.

Index